FATS, OILS, AND SWEETS

by Robin Nelson

first step nonfiction

Lerner Publications Company · Minneapolis

We need to eat many kinds
of food to be **healthy**.

We should not eat a lot of
fats, **oils**, and **sweets**.

Oil is a kind of fat.

Sweets have a lot of sugar.

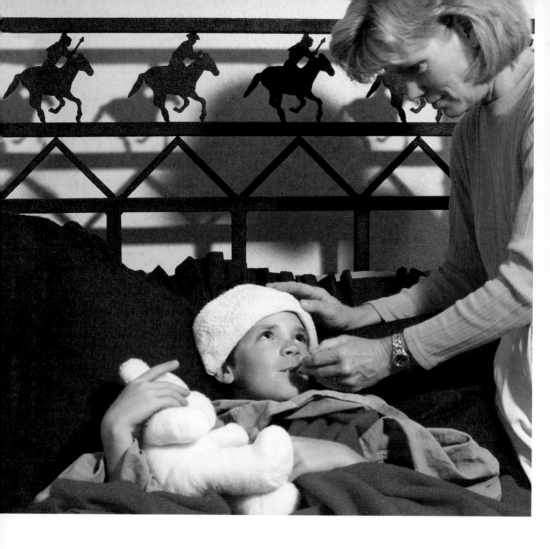

Too much fat and sugar
can make us sick.

Too much fat and sugar
can be **unhealthy**.

There are many snacks in
this group.

We should not eat too
many cookies.

We should not eat too
many french fries.

We should not drink too
much soda.

We can choose healthy
snacks.

We can eat popcorn.

We can eat vegetables.

We can eat fruits.

We can eat yogurt.

Watching what I eat keeps
me healthy.

Fats, Oils, and Sweets
Use Sparingly

Milk, Yogurt, and Cheese Group
2-3 Servings

Vegetable Group
3-5 Servings

Meat, Poultry, Fish, Dry Beans, Eggs, and Nuts Group
2-3 Servings

Fruit Group
2-4 Servings

Bread, Cereal, Rice, and Pasta Group
6-11 Servings

Fats, Oils, and Sweets

The food pyramid shows us how many servings of different foods we should eat every day. Fats, oils, and sweets are at the top of the food pyramid. This part of the pyramid is the smallest because you should not eat very many foods from this group. Many snacks like chips, cookies, candy, and soda belong to this group. The foods in this group taste good, but they have a lot of sugar or fat in them.

Fats, Oils, and Sweets Facts

 The most popular ice cream flavor is vanilla.

 The first chocolate chip cookie was invented by Ruth Graves Wakefield in 1930.

 Americans drink over 13 billion gallons of soft drinks each year.

 Each year, the most candy is sold during Halloween.

 Potato chips are Americans' favorite snack food.

Seven billion pounds of chocolate and candy are manufactured each year in the United States.

 Candy is the number one choice among children for an afternoon snack.

 If all the Easter jellybeans eaten by Americans in one year were lined end to end, they would circle the globe almost three times.

Glossary

 fats – parts of food that give you energy

 healthy – not sick; well

 oils – fatty liquids used in food

 sweets – foods that contain a lot of sugar and taste good

 unhealthy – sick; not well

Index

The photographs in this book are reproduced through the courtesy of: © Todd Strand/IPS, front cover, pp. 3, 4, 5, 8, 9, 11, 12, 13, 15, 17, 22 (top, middle, second from bottom); © PhotoDisc/ Royalty-Free, pp. 2, 7, 10, 22 (second from top); © Corbis Royalty-Free Images, pp. 6, 22 (bottom); © USDA/Bill Tarpenning, p. 14; © Midwest Dairy Association, p. 16.

Illustration on page 18 by Bill Hauser.

Lerner Publications Company
A division of Lerner Publishing Group
241 First Avenue North
Minneapolis, MN 55401 USA

Website address: www.lernerbooks.com

Library of Congress Cataloging-in-Publication Data

Nelson, Robin, 1971–
        Fats, oils, and sweets / by Robin Nelson.
            p.   cm. — (First step nonfiction)
        Summary: An introduction to fats and sweets and the part they play in a healthy diet.
        ISBN: 0–8225–4634–5 (lib. bdg. : alk. paper)
        1. Oils and fats—Juvenile literature. 2. Confectionery—Juvenile literature. 3. Nutrition—Juvenile literature. [1. Oils and fats, Edible. 2. Confectionery. 3. Nutrition.] I. Title.
II. Series.
        TX560.F3 N45 2003
        641.3—dc21   2002013619

Manufactured in the United States of America
1 2 3 4 5 6 – JR – 08 07 06 05 04 03

A Prayer of Thanks

Thank You, God, for all the blessings
You have given me—
For my life and for my joys
And for my family.

A Prayer for My Mom

Dear God, please bless my mother
For she has blessed us all
With love and kind attention
To our problems big and small.
She's always there to give us hugs
And wipe our tears away.
She lets us know how much she
Loves us every single day.
So God, please fill her life with joy
And make her troubles few.
Please give my mother peace of mind
As only You can do.

TURN PAGE

A Prayer for My Dad

Dear God, I'd like to thank you
For giving me my dad,
Who cares so much about me
And who makes me feel so glad,
My dad who makes me smile
And gives me good advice,
My dad who I'd not trade away
For any kind of price,
My dad who says he's blessed with me
When I know all the time,

That I'm the one who's really blessed
To have a dad like mine.
Dear God, please hear my humble prayer.
Please listen to my plea.
Always keep my father safe.
He means so much to me.

TURN PAGE

A Prayer for My Brother

Dear God above, to You I pray,
Please keep my brother safe today.
Protect and lead him far from strife,
Today, tomorrow, all his life.
Please let Your holy glory glow
And steer him from the sinning woes.
Please help him grow and live your plan
To be an upright Christian man.

TURN PAGE

A Prayer for My Sister

Dear Lord above, please hold my sister
Ever in Your heart.
Please help her make decisions
And to live a life that's smart.
Please guide her with Your glory
Through the troubles she may face,
And help her know Your promise
That we Christians all embrace.
Dear Lord, be with my sister
Through the joys and tears of life,
With her career and in her home,
As woman, mom, and wife.

A Prayer for My Grandpa

Dear God, please bless my grandpa
And fill his heart with joy
When he looks back upon his life
To when he was a boy,
And thinks of his own grandpa
And how he loved him so –
That's how I love my grandpa.
Please make sure he always knows.
Dear God, please bless my grandpa
And hold him in Your hand.
Thank you God for grandpa
For he makes my life so grand.

TURN PAGE

A Prayer for My Grandma

Dear God, please bless my grandma
And may she always be
Embraced by every one of us,
Her faithful family.
And may her smile always bloom
Like roses in the spring.
And may her voice ring clear and bright
With every song she sings.
Dear God, I love my grandma,
And I pray she'll always be
Held in Your kind and watchful eye
For all eternity.

TURN PAGE

A Prayer for My Aunt

Dear God, I pray that you will grant
Your blessings on my dearest aunt.
Please ease her woes and make them few.
Please keep her safe and happy, too.
Please fill her life with lots of cheer.
Please look upon my aunt so dear.

A Prayer for My Uncle

Dear God so great, let me relate
Just how I appreciate
My uncle's smile, his humble style,
His gentle heart so kind and mild.
Dear God, please bless and grant success –
I pray for uncle, all the best.

TURN PAGE

A Prayer for My Cousin

Dear Lord, please bless my cousin,
And please fill my cousin's heart
With the feelings of the joy
That life with You imparts.
I pray that Cousin's days are sweet
In life by You bestowed.
Please keep my cousin safe from harm
And on the Christian road.

A Prayer for My Pet

Dear God, I have a pet that I
Would like for You to bless.
It's always there to cheer me up
And bring me happiness.
So won't You kindly keep it safe
And fill its life with play.
My pet means very much to me.
Please bless it all its days.

A Prayer for Family Dinner

Dear God, please hear
my humble prayer.
Thank You for this
meal we share.
We're grateful that
we are so blessed,
When other families
have much less.
Each of us that
gather here,
Give thanks to you,
our Lord so dear.
How much I love
this precious time
With family I'm
so glad is mine.

TURN PAGE

A Prayer for Bedtime

Dear God, before
  I go to sleep,
I pray that You
  will guard and keep
My family in
  Your loving sight,
And keep us safe
  throughout the night.
Please bless us all
  with peaceful dreams,
Snug with faith
  in You Supreme.